Poems for My Best Friend

Collected by **Susie Gibbs**
Illustrated by **Lucy Truman**

OXFORD
UNIVERSITY PRESS

Contents

Poems for My Best Friend

...on Street, Oxford ...

Oxford University Press is a department of the University of Oxford.
It furthers the University's objective of excellence in research, scholarship,
and education by publishing worldwide in

Oxford New York

Auckland Bangkok Buenos Aires Cape Town
Chennai Dar es Salaam Delhi Hong Kong Istanbul
Karachi Kolkata Kuala Lumpur Madrid Melbourne Mexico City Mumbai
Nairobi São Paulo Shanghai Taipei Tokyo Toronto

Oxford is a registered trade mark of Oxford University Press
in the UK and in certain other countries

British Library Cataloguing in Publication Data available

ISBN 0 19 275390 8

1 3 5 7 9 10 8 6 4 2

Typeset by Mary Tudge (Typesetting Services)

Printed in Great Britain

I want to be your friend

Oath of Friendship

SHANG YA!
I want to be your friend
For ever and ever without break or decay.
When the hills are all flat
And the rivers are all dry,
When it lightens and thunders in winter,
When it rains and snows in summer,
When Heaven and Earth mingle—
Not till then will I part from you.

Anon.
(First Century BC) translated by Arthur Waley

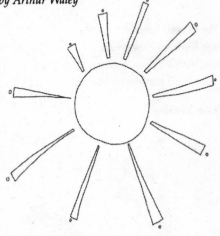

Together

We're bacon and eggs.
We're fried fish and chips.
We're curry and rice.
We're lipstick and lips.

We're baked beans on toast.
We're cake and ice-cream.
We're letter and stamp.
We're kettle and steam.

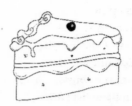

We're water and fish.
We're blanket and bed.
We're saucer and cup.
We're hat and its head.

We're curtain and window.
We're bright shoe and sock.
We're picture and frame.
We're door and strong lock.

We fit well together.
We have no loose ends.
So that's how we know
That we'll always be friends.

John Kitching

Cheese and Chips

We're chalk and cheese
Annoy and please
We're gossip and secret
We're throw it and keep it
We're gulps and sips
We're chocs and chips
We're books and the Net
We're now and not yet
We're sit down and dance
'You bet!' and 'No thanks!'
We're earn it and learn it
We're buy it and burn it
We're girl group and solo
We're on time and no show
We're write and phone
We're smile and moan
We're rush and chill
We're luck and skill
We're scoring and passing
Unique and fashion
We're spend and save
Break the rules and behave
We're ride it and walk
We're quiet and talk
We're cheese and chalk
Who are we?
We're best friends, of course!

Adam Smith

9

I've Had This Shirt

I've had this shirt
that's covered in dirt
for years and years and years.

It used to be red
but I wore it in bed
and it went grey
cos I wore it all day
for years and years and years.

The arms fell off
in the Monday wash
and you can see my vest
through the holes in the chest
for years and years and years.

As my shirt falls apart
I'll keep the bits
in a biscuit tin
on the mantelpiece
for years and years and years.

Michael Rosen

**Friends come in strange disguises
Friends come in all shapes and sizes**

Wardrobe

I've got nothing to wear!
There isn't a thing there
that will do.
It's true: the only good things
aren't clean. And these jeans
are no use. It's not an excuse;
I couldn't go out in *that*:
I'd look like something the cat
had dragged in. Most of this
is only fit for the bin.
I don't know where to begin.
I'd go out and buy something new
except I've got nothing to go in.
I don't know what to do.

Of course! Why didn't I think of it before?
I'll borrow something off you . . .

Adrian Henri

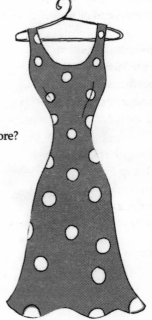

Me and You

Tell me why you're crying,
Tell me why you're sad,
Tell me why you're silent,
Tell me what's so bad.

I've got no one to talk to,
I'm always on my own,
I've got no one to call a friend,
I'm scared and all alone.

Talk to me, I'll listen,
I'm sometimes lonely too,
Together we can beat it,
Together—me and you.

Clive Webster

A poem to keep your spirits up

When you are called names, remember

If bullies mock and reject you
Repeat after the poet, please:
A cat's a wonderful creature
That does not converse with its fleas.

Brian Patten

What are best friends for?

Friends (what are they for?)

Friends are for sharing,
Sweets, money, toys,
Clothes, thoughts, gossip,
Troubles and joys.

Friends are needed
When you're troubled,
Troubles are halved,
Joys are doubled.

Friends are for sharing,
Sweets, money, toys,
Clothes, thoughts, gossip,
But, *definitely not*, boys.

Ian Larmont

Left Out Together

There's the crowd of them again,
So happy and carefree,
Laughing and chatting, going somewhere,
Not including me.
They never say, 'Why don't you come too?'
I wander away and pretend I don't care—
But I do.

You look as though
You might be feeling the same:
Left on the sidelines,
Out of the game . . . ?
You are?
Well, I was wondering whether
We could team up
And both be left out together.

Eric Finney

Friendship starts in many ways

15

I'll always, always be your friend

Friend

I love swimming,
she hates getting wet.
She loves dancing,
I can't work out the steps.
She loves crunchy peanut butter,
I hate the lumps.
I love raspberry ripple ice cream,
she hates the ripple.

But where we're the same,
the bit that people just don't see,
is that I bring out the best in her
and she the best in me.

Anne Wright

Always

You'll always, always
Be my friend.
From year's chill start
Through birdsong spring,
Through summer fruit,
Through falling leaf
Through winter's snowed and icy art,
Through thick and thin,
Through rain and shine,
I'll always, always be your friend,
And know for sure that you'll be mine.

John Kitching

What it takes to be a good friend . . .

Great mate
Talk straight
Gossip bearer
Trouble sharer
Staunch defender
Text sender
Town shopper
Clothes swapper
Tear drier
Present buyer
Party thrower
Secrets knower
Best friends for ever
Fall out never!

Catharine Boddy

Recipe for Good Friends

Take:

  2 people (any age or size)
  2 portions of mutual admiration
  1 sense of humour (shared)
  a pinch of trust
  1 or 2 common interests (optional, to taste)

Throw all the ingredients together and keep mixing
  at regular intervals.
Stir in a couple of wonderful moments and then
  add 1 or 2 bad times to strengthen.
Leave to set for as long as possible.
Take out and serve at any social occasion or may be enjoyed simply
  on its own.

N.B. If properly handled should keep indefinitely.

Jane Saddler

Mobile-Phoning Sally All About It

Well, that's nothing! I came home
from yours last night ('*Back
by nine or you're in for it!*' Dad said.)
and you won't believe,
there they were on the couch
snogging! Our Paula and her feller!
(She calls him her *beau*!)
Snogging! Well, I *mean*! Horrible
and slobbery. Like a baby with
porridge all over its face. I said,
'*I'll tell our dad!*' And our Paula said,
'*Go on then. I don't give a monkey's!*'

I opened the door into the next room
and—no, honest!—there they were,
my own father and mother

on the couch . . .

'They *weren't*!' They *were*!

He had his arm round her and . . .

Matt Simpson

You can tell your best friend anything

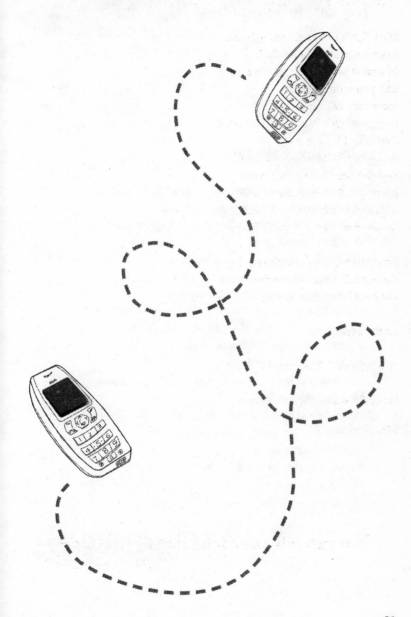

Lip, Zip, Friendship

My best mate's turned me into a talkaholic.
Our lips could not zip if you paid them.
In class, our teacher rolls her eyes like a fruit machine
Trying to keep us quiet.
But words will not do as they are told
And disguise themselves in a whisper
That tiptoes from my mouth to my mate.
This is how we relate.
Clothes and shoes are the subject we study.
We could sit SATs on What to Wear.
In the canteen we catch up.
Lunch on the latest about boys and the box and bands.
My mate, she understands.
When we get home, conversation continues on the phone.
Mum goes mad, can't see our need to natter.
Sleepover's the best—
It's an all-night-spout-till-Mum-shouts-out job.
I can tell her anything.
Friendship is a blessing with my best mate.

Andrew Fusek Peters and Polly Peters

This Thing

There's this thing
we could do—
you be me
I'll be you

We'll swap lives
we'll swap clothes
we'll swap shoes
we'll swap homes

Eat my breakfast
I'll eat yours
tease my brother
I'll tease yours

We'll swap Mums
we'll swap Dads
we'll swap homework
we'll swap cats

Read my diary
I'll read yours
share our secrets

second thoughts—

NO WAY!!!!

James Carter

A Poem for My Cat

You're black and sleek and beautiful
What a pity your best friends won't tell you
Your breath smells of Kit-E-Kat.

Adrian Henri

Friendship

There once were two back-country geezers
Who got porcupine quills in their sneezers.
    They sat beak to beak
    For more than a week
Working over each other with tweezers.

John Ciardi

To Be

Be good,
Be bad,
But be sincere.
Be happy,
Be sad,
But please be clear.
Be sure,
Be certain,
But to the end:
Be constant,
Be always,
My best friend.

Pat Gadsby

... or are they?

Stopgap

Julie says she's my very best friend,
But I don't need to be told:
Julie will be my very best friend
Until Sue gets over her cold.

Pat Gadsby

And then she came along . .

There we were
Thick as thieves
Best friends
Holding hands, arms round each other
And then she came along

There we were
Passing notes in secret codes
Sharing secrets
Whispering, giggling
And then she came along

There we were
Round at each other's houses
Laughing at our special jokes
Dressing up for parties together
And then she came along

She came along
And suddenly I was dull
We'd played all my games before
My jokes didn't make you laugh
I wish she'd never come along

She came along
And you only had eyes for her
You knew all my secrets
The nooks and crannies of my house
Held no surprises

I wish she'd never come along

Beverley Johnson

Best Friends

Best friends tell you secrets
Best friends always play
Best friends send you postcards
When they go away.

Best friends guess your thinking
Best friends read your eyes
Best friends notice right away
If you're telling lies.

Best friends say they're sorry
Best friends say they care
Best friends may be absent
But they're always there.

Steve Turner

**Best friends are there
when you need them**

There For You

You were there when Sven hurt me
When he said what he said
And your words reassured me
I was *not* over-fed

And when Sven two-timed me
With that girl from Stoke
You said, It's not your fault
It's just typical bloke

You were there when Sven dumped me
I held onto your arm
You led me from chaos
To an island of calm

So, know in your heart
I'll be there for you when
You need reassurance
Now that *you're* dating Sven

Roger Stevens

Phyllis

You knew me when I didn't know myself
And when I lose myself you find me.
Whenever things get bad
And I forget the good I've had,
You help remind me.

I tell you of my joys. My joys increase.
I tell my sorrows. They diminish.
And when I want to quit
You keep me going, bit by bit,
Until I finish.

Friendship is an art and you have made
The act of friendship your great art form.
I know that I can bear
The biggest chill because you're there
To keep my heart warm.

Judith Viorst

Friendship is an art

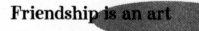

Best Friend

When there's just one square
of chocolate left . . .
she shares,
she gives me half.

When thunder growls like an angry bear
and I shiver and shake
beneath my chair . . .
she won't laugh.

When I'm grumpy or cross
or spotty or sad,
when I whine or boss . . .
she stays.

When things aren't fair
and I hurt inside,
when I just want to hide . . .
she's there,
always.

Judith Nicholls

You find out who your friends are

We all admired her.
She was in the year above us.
Glamorous.
So when she picked me out to mock
And said *that thing*
In front of all the others
Everyone fell silent.
Numb, too shocked to cry
I felt as if she'd slapped me.
Nightmare of an afternoon.
No one said, 'You OK?'
But when I walked out through the gate
You were the one
Who walked with me.
My mate.

Sue Cowling

**Best friends stick up
for each other**

With

To shop with
And share with
And show off your hair with

To chat with
And cheer with
And chase away fear with

To plan with
And play with
Be pleased you can stay with

To trick with
And trust with
Completely and just with

Your friend.

Daphne Kitching

Us Two

Wherever I am, there's always Pooh,
There's always Pooh and Me.
Whatever I do, he wants to do,
'Where are you going today?' says Pooh:
'Well, that's very odd 'cos I was too.
Let's go together,' says Pooh, says he.
'Let's go together,' says Pooh.

'What's twice eleven?' I said to Pooh,
('Twice what?' said Pooh to Me.)
'I *think* it ought to be twenty-two.'
'Just what I think myself,' said Pooh.
'It wasn't an easy sum to do,
But that's what it is,' said Pooh, said he.
'That's what it is,' said Pooh.

'Let's look for dragons,' I said to Pooh.
'Yes, let's,' said Pooh to Me.
We crossed the river and found a few—
'Yes, those are dragons all right,' said Pooh.
'As soon as I saw their beaks I knew.
That's what they are,' said Pooh, said he.
'That's what they are,' said Pooh.

'Let's frighten the dragons,' I said to Pooh.
'That's right,' said Pooh to Me.
'*I'm* not afraid,' I said to Pooh,
And I held his paw and I shouted, 'Shoo!
Silly old dragons!'—and off they flew.
'I wasn't afraid,' said Pooh, said he,
'I'm *never* afraid with you.'

So wherever I am, there's always Pooh,
There's always Pooh and Me.
'What would I do?' I said to Pooh,
'If it wasn't for you,' and Pooh said: 'True,
It isn't much fun for One, but Two
Can stick together,' says Pooh, says he.
'That's how it is,' says Pooh.

A. A. Milne

Secret

Tell me your secret.
I promise not to tell.
I'll guard it safely at the bottom of a well.

Tell me your secret.
Tell me, tell me, please.
I won't breathe a word, not even to the bees.

Tell me your secret.
It will be a pebble in my mouth.
Not even the sea can make me spit it out.

John Agard

Best friends keep secrets

Thick as Thieves

You wouldn't think
to see that pair
they'd been tearing at
each other's hair.

You wouldn't guess
to hear them speak
they'd screamed abuses
all last week.

Thick as thieves.
Forever friends
is how their quarrel
always ends.

Ann Bonner

Vexed Text

remember wen I we
nt away u stole m
y boyfriend jack?
well now uve gone
2 florida im gonn
a steal him back.

Marcus Parry

Best friends *don't* steal your boyfriend

Betrayal

Tracy—I saw you by the school gate
Talking to Darren Brown,
You and he were laughing
I walked home feeling down.

You know I've liked him for ages,
You must have been able to see
All this time I've been trying
To get him to notice me.

This happened before, with Matthew,
I told you I thought he was nice
You set out to get him the very next day,
It was obvious you didn't think twice.

So I'm writing you this to tell you,
I don't want to be friends any more,
Because I think that stealing my boyfriend
Is not what best friends are for.

Anne Logan

Growing

My best friend, she isn't. Well, not any more
for best friends are two . . . and that's what we swore

but two became three
and three was a crowd.
Three can't be best friends. It isn't allowed.

but two became three

So Ann Other joined us
and four friends were we—
more balanced like that. We did all agree

that four can be better
at friends than can five.

Two's company

This being 'best friends' business
couldn't survive
for odds were against it
when
six girls
or seven,
eight of them,
nine,
even ten
or eleven
jostled
for power
where
two girls began.
*

We two were best friends
and now we're a gang.

Gina Douthwaite

$$x+y=?-z= ?$$

Arithmetic

She takes ten and divides it by three:
it breaks, hard-edged, echoing.

She divides a wet sky by a high window,
she wants to add a radio, take away the teacher.
The day isn't working out right.

She's given up caring about correct answers.
That makes the sums easy. So easy it bores her.

She measures the drawn-out length of the lesson
against the chipped edge of the desk—and still
finds it's too long till the bell.

Love/hate/love/hate/love/hate

She counts up her friends and subtracts
her enemies. Now that's interesting

but difficult, difficult.

Dave Calder

x friends $+$

y friends

$-z$ enemies $=$

???? ?   ?   ?

Green

Sitting in the launderette
Delight and Carol, side by side,
Watch their washing whirl around,
Wishing it was done and dried.

Delight begins to paint her nails
While Carol sits and stares.
First vivid green, then silver specks,
To match the shoes she wears.

Then Carol says, 'That Stan of yours,
He's quite a guy, you know.
We met him down the Rink last week—
That day you didn't go.

He really fancies Eth, he does,
Don't say you hadn't heard.'
Delight begins to paint her toes,
She doesn't say a word.

Friends you could do without

'I think he asked her for a date—
Of course, I couldn't swear—
He never took his eyes off her,
That day that you weren't there.'

Delight gets slowly to her feet,
Walks up to Carol's machine,
Tips the paint in the top of it,
And watches her washing turn green.

Jennifer Curry

Best friends just don't work like that

Being Friends with Penny

Everyone wants to be friends with Penny,
She's got us all on her string.
She's the school's golden girl, brilliant at lessons
And sports—and everything.

She's tall and the teachers love her
But she said to me today,
'If you want us to be best friends, Rebecca,
You'll have to do as I say.'

Then her dazzling smile was turned on me
And her golden hair was tossed.
Best friendships just don't work like that.
I told her to get lost.

Eric Finney

The Argument

Did!
Didn't!
Could!
Couldn't!
Was!
Wasn't!
Should!
Shouldn't!
Can!
Can't!
Would!
Wouldn't!
Wouldn't what?
Can't remember . . .

Sue Hardy-Dawson

Gone Pear-shaped

Best friends we were for ages,
There was never the slightest row,
The Inseparables everyone called us:
Well, it's all gone pear-shaped now.

It used to be giggle and gossip and chat,
Sleepovers and secrets to share.
Now she's off with the school's sports hero
With his David Beckham hair.

They hang out together all the time,
She calls him *My Best Buddy*.
She even supports his football matches,
And her nice shoes get all muddy.

Are you my friend or aren't you?

She doesn't exactly brush me off
But it's not like it used to be.
'Not available,' she says with a smile
When I ask her round for tea.

I've told her it's quite ridiculous,
It'll come to a sticky end.
No way can it be like it was with us—
You can't have a *boy* for best friend.

Eric Finney

Friends Again?

When snow melts to slush
And noise becomes hush
When smile answers frown
And upside turns down,
When bitter tastes sweet
And both our ends meet
Then a flash in the pan
Will be what we began.

When each finds the other
And lose is discover,
When feeble feels strong
And short stretches long,
When head rules the heart
And we make a fresh start
Then if No or if Yes
Will be anyone's guess.

John Mole

Yes/no/yes/no/yes/no

Are you my friend or aren't you?

Are you my friend or aren't you?
I don't think friendship's a game.
Monday we skipped down our street arm in arm,
Today you're giggly with Jane.

Are you my friend or aren't you?
Will I ever know anyone well?
You laughed yesterday at the joke I made,
Today you laughed when I fell.

Are you my friend or aren't you?
How to tell truth from a lie?
On Tuesday you lent me your best felt-tipped pens,
Now I just can't catch your eye.

Are you my friend or aren't you?
There are so many things I don't know.
Where does the sun set, the east or the west?
How do I stop feeling low?

Are you my friend or aren't you?
You've made things so hard I can't guess.
Perhaps it's a question I wouldn't be asking,
If the answer was yes.

Trevor Parsons

It is a Puzzle

My friend
Is not my friend any more.
She has secrets from me
And goes about with Tracy Hackett.

I would
Like to get her back,
Only do not want to say so.
So I pretend
To have secrets from her
And go about with Alice Banks.

But what bothers me is,
Maybe *she* is pretending
And would like *me* back,
Only does not want to say so.

In which case
Maybe it bothers her
That *I* am pretending.

How can we be friends . . . .

But if we are both pretending,
Then really we are friends
And do not know it.

On the other hand,
How can we be friends
And have secrets from each other
And go about with other people?

My friend
Is not my friend any more,
Unless she is pretending.
I cannot think what to do.
It is a puzzle.

Allan Ahlberg

. . . and have secrets from each other?

Bird

Sometimes being your best friend
Makes me feel like a little bird
With my beak stretched open
Ruffling my feathers,
Hungry.

Lucinda Jacob

The Quarrel

Jan and Gemma quarrelled.
Gemma spoke about Jan's dog
as 'only a mongrel'.

Jan said, 'If not really
nasty, that was unkind.'

Gemma said, '*Mongrel* is
neither nasty nor unkind.'

'Yes,' Jan insisted:
'mongrel is not a kind word.
Especially when
"only" is attached to it.'

'Perhaps,' Gemma said. 'But
not *terrible, terrible*, is it?'

Jan said: 'Call my dog
"a mixed breed", that is fine.
But—not *only a mongrel*".'

Saying sorry

Gemma said: 'All right, Jan.
Suppose—I give you a fudge.'

Jan said: 'That would be friendly.
Especially—if "sorry"
is written on it, in ink.

And you give me another
one, to give back to you.
With "sorry" on it in ink.'

'Splendid,' Gemma said. 'Splendid.'
Silent, for a little while,
both girls ate a fudge, carefully.

James Berry

I'm really sorry

You

You
I don't like you
you're not nice you
you're dead tight you
why've we got to
do what you want you
I'm right off

You
think you're great you
everybody hates you
nobody rates you
you call names you
spoil the games you
we're not mates

You
don't share you
it's not fair you
I don't care you
can clear off you
had enough of you
so there

You
you can get lost you
you're not the boss you
needn't think y'are because you
you're not see
so are you gonna call for me
or what?

David Horner

Apology

It's hard to say 'I'm sorry,'
Although I'm feeling sorry.
The 's' always sticks in my throat.
And 'I made a big mistake'
Would produce a bellyache
That might last till I was old enough to vote.

'Please forgive me' sounds real good.
And I'd say it if I could,
But between the 'forgive' and the 'please'
I would have to go to bed
With a pounding in my head
And a very shaky feeling in my knees.

'I was wrong' seems oh so right.
But it gives me such a fright
That my 'was' always turns into 'ain't'.
So I hope you'll take this rhyme
As my way of saying 'I'm
Really sorry.' Now excuse me while I faint.

Judith Viorst

The Blood Pact

As little kids we cut our fingers
Mixed the blood and let it lie:
Said it was a pact of friendship,
Vowed our friendship would not die.
Now I am all old and hoary,
You are withered like a stick;
Still that pact holds true between us,
Hey, that mix of blood was thick!

Philippa Roberts

For Ever

Will we be friends for ever,
ever and a day?
Will we be friends when other friends
have left and gone their way?
Will we be best friends
when we're ninety-three
and will I still like you best?
Will you like me?
We can't see the future;
nobody knows how
but we can both be happy
that we are best friends now.

Marian Swinger

The only disagreement you will be happy to have with your best friend

My best friend is better than yours
And I can prove it's true.
Because your best friend is only me
And my best friend is you.

Elaine Johnson

Be my best friend

May You Always

May your smile be ever present
May your skies be always blue
May your path be ever onward
May your heart be ever true

May your dreams be full to bursting
May your steps be always sure
May the fire within your soul
Blaze on for evermore

May you live to meet ambition
May you strive to pass each test
May you find the love your life deserves
May you always have the best

May your happiness be plentiful
May your regrets be few
May you always be my best friend
May you always . . . just be you

Paul Cookson

Acknowledgements

Every effort has been made to trace and contact copyright holders before publication and we are grateful to all those who have granted us permission. We apologize for any inadvertent errors and will be pleased to rectify these at the earliest opportunity.

John Agard: 'Secret' from *Get Back Pimple* (Puffin, 1997), copyright © John Agard 1997, reprinted by kind permission of John Agard c/o Caroline Sheldon Literary Agency.
Allan Ahlberg: 'It is a Puzzle' from *Please Mrs Butler* (Kestral, 1983), copyright © Allan Ahlberg 1983, reprinted by permission of Penguin UK.
James Berry: 'The Quarrel' from *A Nest Full of Stars* (Macmillan Children's Books, 2002), copyright © James Berry 2002, reprinted by permission of PFD (www.pfd.co.uk) on behalf of James Berry.
John Ciardi: 'Friendship' from *The Hopeful Trout and Other Limericks* by John Ciardi, copyright © 1989 Myra J. Ciardi. Reprinted by permission of Houghton Mifflin Company. All rights reserved.
Adrian Henri: 'Wardrobe' from *Collected Poems* (Alison & Busby, 1986), copyright © Adrian Henri 1986 and 'Poem For My Cat' from *The Phantom Lollipop Lady* (Methuen, 1986), copyright © Adrian Henri 1986, both reprinted by permission of the author c/o Rogers, Coleridge & White Ltd., 20 Powis Mews, London, W11 1JN.
A. A. Milne: 'Us Two' from *Now We Are Six* (Methuen, 1928), copyright © A. A. Milne 1928, reprinted by permission of the publisher, Egmont Books Ltd, London.
John Mole: 'Friends Again?' from *The Wonder Dish* (Oxford University Press, 2002), copyright © John Mole 2002, reprinted by permission of the author.
Judith Nicholls: 'Best Friend' from *Someone I Like* (Barefoot Books, 2000) copyright © Judith Nicholls 2000, reprinted by permission of the author.
Brian Patten: 'When you are called names, remember' from *Juggling with Gerbils* (Puffin, 2000), copyright © Brian Patten 2000, reprinted by permission of the author c/o Rogers, Coleridge & White Ltd., 20 Powis Mews, London, W11 1JN.
Andrew Fusek Peters and Polly Peters: 'Lip, Zip, Friendship' from *Sadderday & Funday* (Hodder Wayland, 2001), copyright © Andrew Fusek Peters and Polly Peters 2001, reprinted by permission of the authors.
Michael Rosen: 'I've Had This Shirt' from *Mind Your Own Business* (Deutsch, 1974), copyright © Michael Rosen 1974, reprinted by permission of PFD (www.pfd.co.uk) on behalf of Michael Rosen.